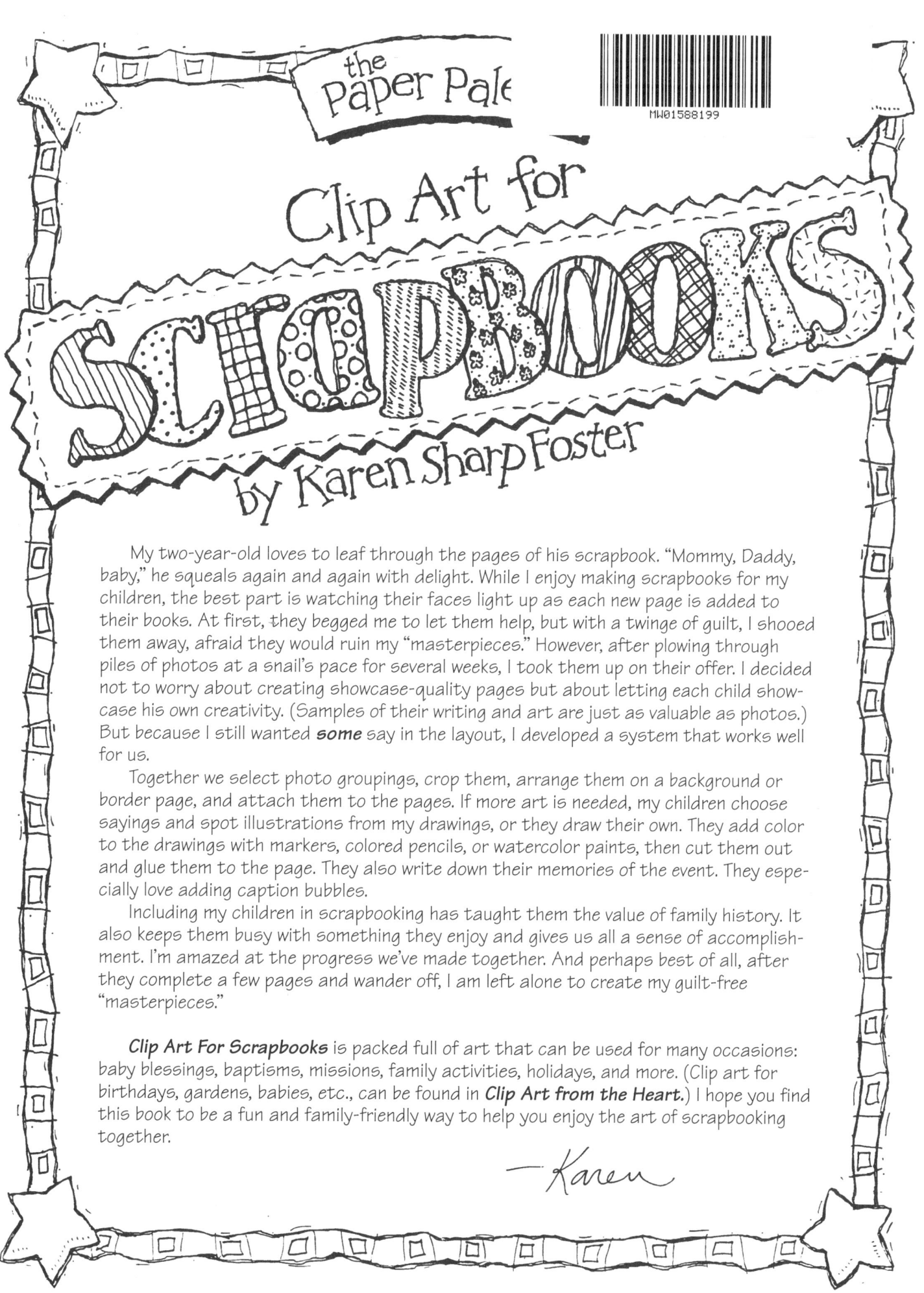

the Paper Pale[tte]
Clip Art for Scrapbooks
by Karen Sharp Foster

My two-year-old loves to leaf through the pages of his scrapbook. "Mommy, Daddy, baby," he squeals again and again with delight. While I enjoy making scrapbooks for my children, the best part is watching their faces light up as each new page is added to their books. At first, they begged me to let them help, but with a twinge of guilt, I shooed them away, afraid they would ruin my "masterpieces." However, after plowing through piles of photos at a snail's pace for several weeks, I took them up on their offer. I decided not to worry about creating showcase-quality pages but about letting each child showcase his own creativity. (Samples of their writing and art are just as valuable as photos.) But because I still wanted *some* say in the layout, I developed a system that works well for us.

Together we select photo groupings, crop them, arrange them on a background or border page, and attach them to the pages. If more art is needed, my children choose sayings and spot illustrations from my drawings, or they draw their own. They add color to the drawings with markers, colored pencils, or watercolor paints, then cut them out and glue them to the page. They also write down their memories of the event. They especially love adding caption bubbles.

Including my children in scrapbooking has taught them the value of family history. It also keeps them busy with something they enjoy and gives us all a sense of accomplishment. I'm amazed at the progress we've made together. And perhaps best of all, after they complete a few pages and wander off, I am left alone to create my guilt-free "masterpieces."

Clip Art For Scrapbooks is packed full of art that can be used for many occasions: baby blessings, baptisms, missions, family activities, holidays, and more. (Clip art for birthdays, gardens, babies, etc., can be found in **Clip Art from the Heart**.) I hope you find this book to be a fun and family-friendly way to help you enjoy the art of scrapbooking together.

—Karen

Copyright © 1997 by Karen Sharp Foster

All rights reserved. Permission is granted **with purchase of book** to copy individual pages for personal use. No part of this book may be reproduced in any form or by any means for commercial use without permission in writing from the publisher, Bookcraft, Inc., 1848 West 2300 South, Salt Lake City, Utah 84119.

Bookcraft is a registered trademark of Bookcraft, Inc.

ISBN 1-57008-352-5

First Printing, 1997

Printed in the United States of America

Instructions

Note: To create scrapbook pages with the art in this book, use acid-free paper, glue, etc. Keep all finished scrapbook pages in clear archival page protectors.

Adding Color

The clip art in this book can be copied onto colored paper or cardstock and used without adding color. However, if you choose to add color, there are many acid-free markers, colored pencils, watercolor pencils, and paints available.

I prefer watercolor paints because they are surprisingly fast and easy to use. You can swish the paint on quickly or spend more time adding detail and shadows. I use high quality watercolors, painted on white or light-colored cardstock. To avoid wrinkling when painting large areas, tape the paper to a Masonite board by running masking tape along the edges. Remove the tape carefully when paint is completely dry. If you want paint to go to the edge of your page, copy onto larger cardstock, paint, then trim to 8½" x 11". When painting small areas taping is not necessary.

Squeeze paint into the wells of a palette (a dinner plate will also work). Use a quality medium-size pointed brush. Dilute the paint by dipping the brush in water, then in the paint. (If using watercolor pencils, rub the wet brush on the tip of your pencil.) The more water on your brush, the lighter the color and more transparent the paint. It's best to start light and add darker paint later if needed. It's also fun to use colors that match the colors in the photos. Test the paint on a piece of scrap paper. Start at the top or side of the object and paint to the opposite side in a continuous back-and-forth motion. To create dimension, the top of the object should be lighter and the bottom darker. For depth, swish a more concentrated shadow of the same color—or gray—along the bottom of the object. Add a bit of white with a colored pencil on the top edge of the object after the paint has dried. I like to paint a light gray, sepia, or complementary colored shadow all the way around the object to make it appear to pop off the page.

Use paper towels to dry your brush after each rinsing and to dab excess paint. If paint goes on too dark blot it with a paper towel. Repeat by painting the area again with straight water and blotting. This can lift off unwanted darkness. Avoid rubbing the paper. Acrylic paints or colored pencil can be used for touch-up or more opaque coloring.

Keep several copies of the page you're working on nearby so you won't be nervous about messing up—you can always start over. Don't worry about going outside the lines—that rule is an elementary school fallacy. Going outside the lines is "in." If desired, trim ⅛" to ¼" around the edge of your painted page and mount on another color (see back cover).

Spot Illustrations and Pattern Papers

The spot illustrations in this book can be used as you would use stickers. Keep copies handy to decorate your page layouts. I add color then cut them out the quick way—wiggly around the edges instead of right on the lines. Attach them to the scrapbook page with an acid-free glue stick. You can also create, ahead of time, your own fully designed pages. First, decide where the photos and art will go, then attach the art to white paper and make several copies of the new pages. Color them and decorate with photos. This creates pages where all the art is permanent. Many of the larger border illustrations can be copied at a smaller size and used as "stickers" to decorate a corresponding page.

The spot illustrations can also be used to create your own borders. Place illustrations in one or more of the corners or across the bottom of white paper. Draw your own border around the edges or use border segments from this book between and around the illustrations. Photocopy your designs.

The two full-pattern pages in this book can be copied onto a variety of colors of cardstock or paper to keep on hand for backgrounds or frames. A tiny portion around the edges of these pages will not copy but can be trimmed.

MY BLESSING WAY

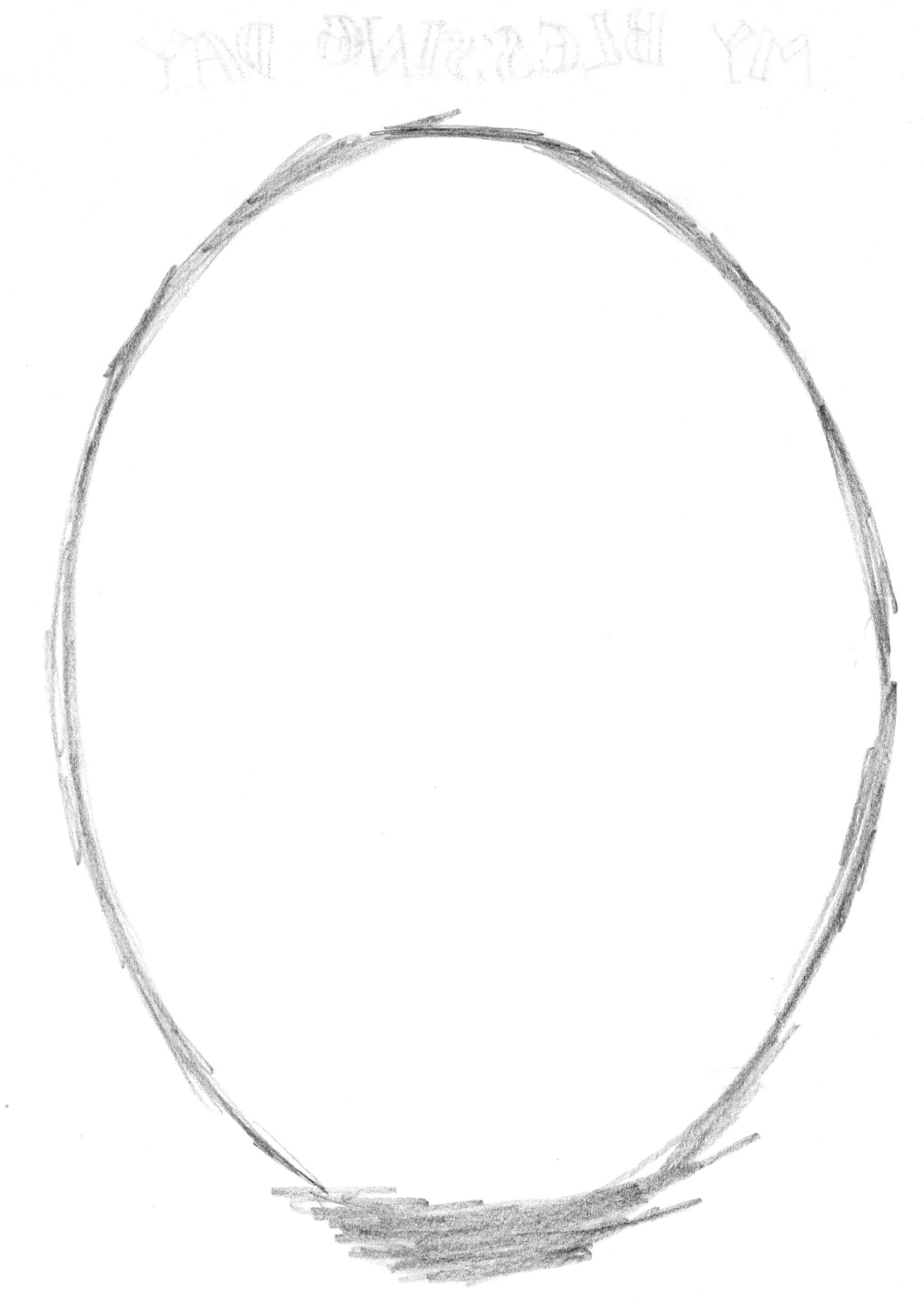

Our family is forever

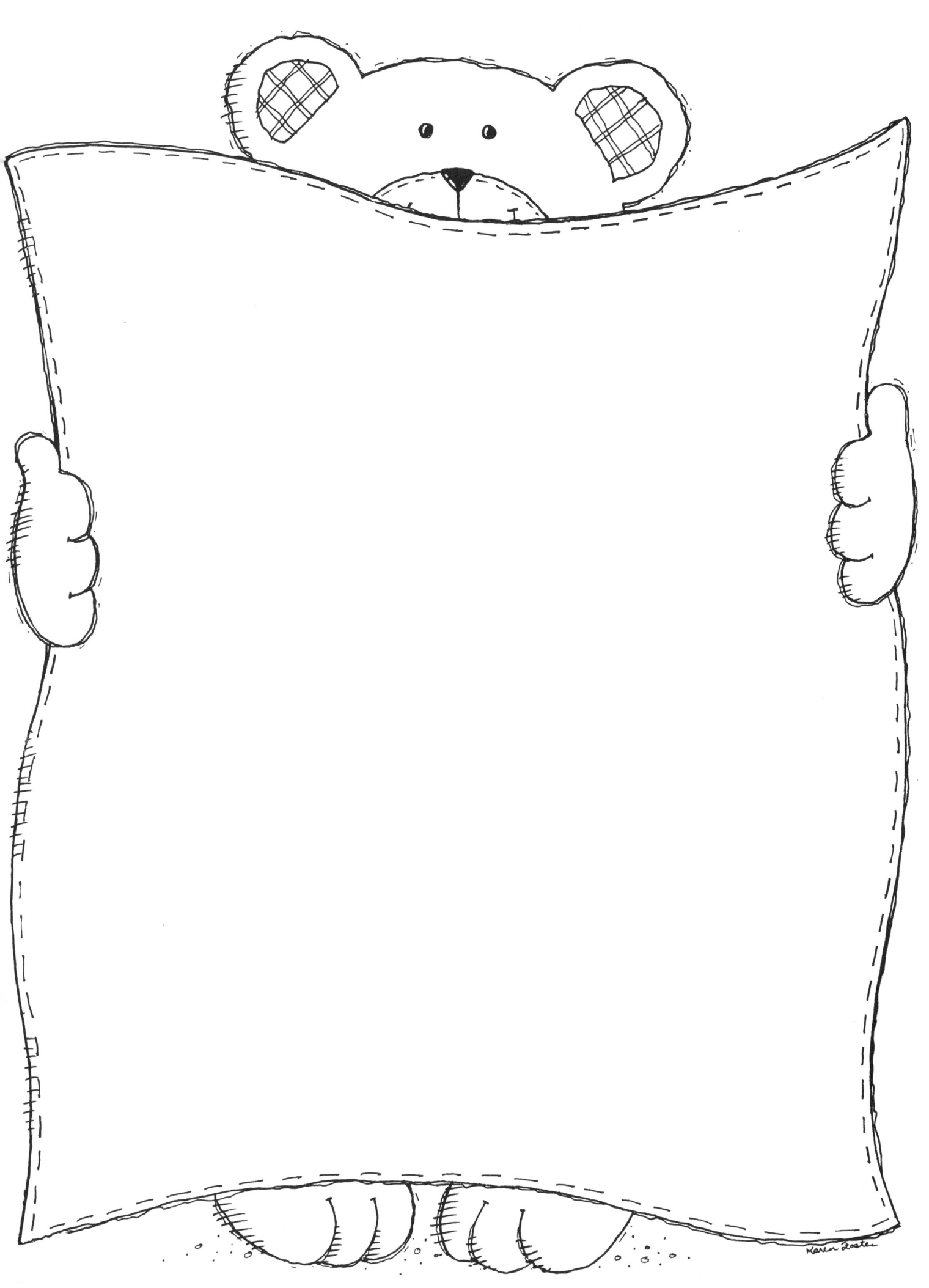

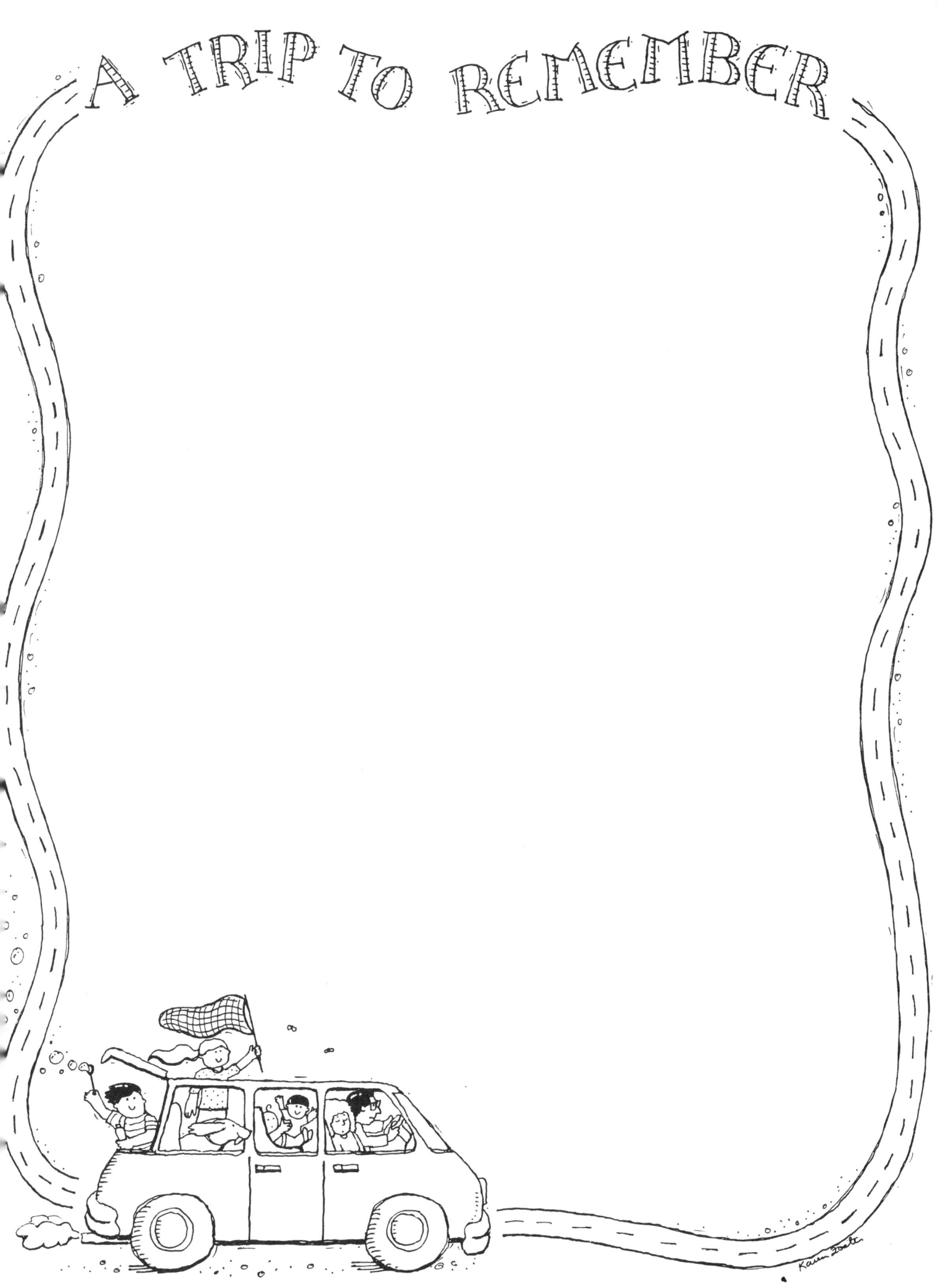

MY HOMECOMING
MY FAREWELL

Missionary Moments

Mission Memories

O that I were an angel...

Lengthen Your Stride

My Mission Call

From: The Prophet
To: The Missionary

the CRAZY days of summer!

God bless America!

let freedom ring!

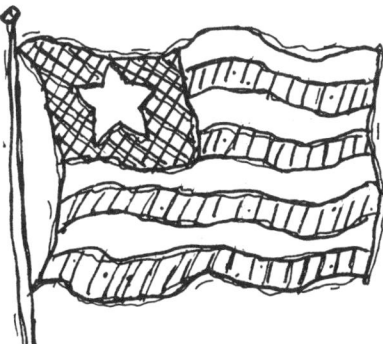

summer-time fun!

look who's monkeyin' around!

Roar and slither,
Squawk and coo,
Things are happening
At the zoo!

Cuddles and Hugs

just "lion" around

Growin' oh so tall

Look who's in the Zoo

Congrats!

Cute as a button

Sleepin' on the job

Makin' Music!

Dance your heart out!

Life is Ruff!

Love is to share

I'm purrr-fect!

Let every heart prepare him room

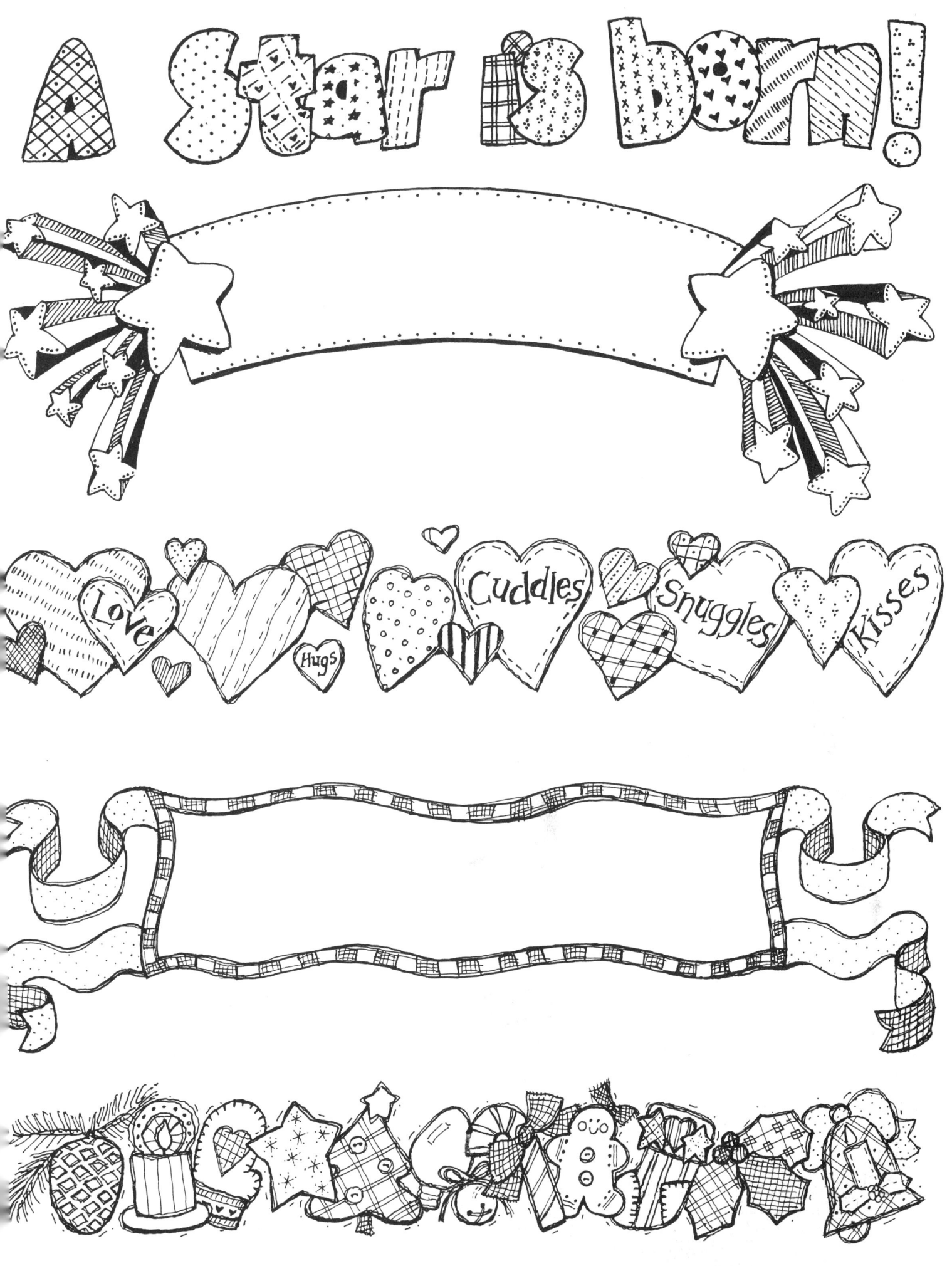

Make copies of each calendar month on acid-free paper or cardstock. Paint if desired. Mark the days by writing small numbers in the corners of each box.

Copy and cut out the spot drawings on the following page and attach them to the appropriate days with a glue stick. Some drawings are blank so you can write in your own ideas. Keep completed pages in scrapbook.

January
February
March
April
May
June

July
August
September
October
November
December

a star is born | comes home | Long nap! | special visitor | smiles | sleeps through night | drinks from a bottle | baby's blessing | reaches for things | recognizes people!

plays with toys | sits | crawls | 1st steps | a tooth pops through | gives a kiss | eats with a spoon | eats real food | drinks from a cup | likes ice cream

| understands "No" | haircut | outing | | sings | 1st trip | first word is: ___ | claps hands

1 month old | 2 months old | 3 months old | 4 months old | 5 months old | 6 months old | 7 months old | 8 months old | 9 months old | 10 months old | 11 months old

1st Birthday | New Year's Eve | Valentine's Day | Easter | St. Patrick's Day | 4th of July! | Halloween | Thanksgiving | Christmas